SANTA BARBARA STYLE

DATE DUE

DEMCO

SANTA BARBARA STYLE

KATHRYN MASSON

Principal Photography by
JAMES CHEN

RIZZOLI
NEW YORK

First published in the United States of America in
2001 by
Rizzoli International Publications, Inc.
300 Park Avenue South, New York, NY 10010

Copyright © 2001 Rizzoli International
Publications, Inc.
Text copyright © 2001 Kathryn Masson
Photography copyright (except as indicated below)
© 2001 James Chen
© 2001 Tim Street-Porter (pp. 150-161)
© 2001 Kathryn Masson (pp. 168-169)

ISBN: 0847823741
LC: 2001086015

Front cover: Ca' di Sopra (p. 46)
Back cover: Lotusland (p. 104)

Page 1: Iron lamp detail, El Paseo (p. 12)

*Frontispiece: A symmetrical landscape design of the
pool area enhances the formal bearing of La Quinta
(p. 126), a 1920s Montecito mansion designed by
Carleton Winslow, Sr.*

Pages 4–5: Vineyard, Pompeiian Court (p. 164)

Designed by Abigail Sturges

Distributed by St. Martin's Press

Printed and bound in Singapore

*To my mom, Birdie,
and the memory of my dad,
David Masson (1920-1997).*

*To my friend Patricia,
and the memory of her husband,
David Gebhard (1927-1996).*

And to my husband David Pashley.

Contents

Santa Barbara's Beginnings: Civic and commercial properties of Santa Barbara

Previous spread: A tiled plaque at the Four Seasons Biltmore Hotel depicts a map of Santa Barbara.

What makes Santa Barbara so special? Many coastal towns of California have the same climate and naturally beautiful environment, as well as the influence of Spain and Mexico in their culture and architecture. Many also have breathtaking views of the coastal foothills that make such a soothing backdrop to white-washed houses with red-tile roofs, where a stunning variety of colorful foliage is in bloom year round. And all of these towns are also endowed with the glorious, ever-present Pacific Ocean. But among all of them, Santa Barbara is unique.

Charmingly reminiscent of an old Spanish town, Santa Barbara exudes a sense of mystery and whimsy enhanced by its striking architecture and lush Mediterranean landscape. Its spirit blends the tranquil quality of a mythical, romantic past with the liveliness of a modern California beach town. The enigmatic Santa Barbara style is the result of many things: its historic, masterful architecture; the legacies left by influential, visionary, and philanthropic citizens; and its enduring community spirit that celebrates life to the fullest. The city that has developed over the past two hundred years, especially through the creative genius of its early twentieth-century builders, reflects the culmination of its citizens' grand vision and passionate desire to create an ideal place — their Eden in California.

On a clear day, the Channel Islands rise mystically out of the ocean: a vision the Chumash, whose predecessors can be traced to 11,000 b.c.e., saw daily. Their villages spanned the coast from Malibu to San Luis Obispo, but they thrived in the area with a proliferation of mountain streams, a plentiful supply of seafood, and a mild climate — an area that is now Santa Barbara.

Juan Rodriguez Cabrillo claimed California's lands for the King of Spain in 1542, but European possession of the golden state was not fully achieved until over two centuries later. It came when agents of the cross and the crown braved the wilderness, determined to convert the indigenous people and settle the coveted land before other European powers could prevail. Spain chose Santa Barbara as the site for one of its four military strongholds in Alta California, and established the Royal Presidio in 1782. The Santa Barbara mission, one of twenty-one in California, was founded in 1786.

From the beginning of the Spanish era to American control of California in 1848, Santa Barbara remained a small pueblo of adobes. The earliest Anglos, captains and sailors from New England trading ships, arrived in the first decades of the nineteenth century. Charmed by the small town's welcoming nature, they often intermarried with the daughters of the Spanish land holders and adopted the alluring, Barbareno lifestyle. In 1849 the California gold rush brought waves of fortune seekers into the western territories. With this great influx, the quaint Spanish town of Santa Barbara quickly grew, and its character changed drastically. In a few short years, it came to resemble other American towns, where prototypes from the east were used to set streets on a grid system and transform the adobe landscape largely into one of Victorian wooden structures.

Santa Barbara's defining moment was imminent, however. In 1887 the railroad connected Los Angeles to Santa Barbara and in 1901 the line was extended north to San Francisco. Santa Barbara was now more readily accessible to travelers. Through heavy national advertising, it had gained a reputation as a health spa, thanks to the natural hot springs in Montecito. Conditions were right for business opportunities that would change the town forever. A 36-acre plot of downtown, beachfront property was purchased by Los Angeles-based Milo Potter, a builder of grand, luxury hotels; and in January, 1903, the enormous and posh, mission style Potter Hotel opened with rooms for 1,000 guests. It immediately began to receive the elite from all over the world for the winter season, and from that time on Santa Barbara was put on the map as a resort town for the rich and famous.

In the meantime, from the 1870s on, Montecito Valley, down the coast and adjacent to Santa Barbara, was developing into an agricultural community. Although the valley had long sustained the Spanish and Mexican families who had settled there, this original land-grant acreage was now purchased and farmed by men, mostly from the east, who sought a healthy climate and had also discovered the good soil and perfect growing conditions of this paradise. Rich alluvial deposits in the floodplains, coupled with a climate very similar to that of the Mediterranean, with which Santa Barbara shares latitude, produced varied and bountiful crops. Pioneering nurserymen raised thousands of fruit and nut trees of different varieties, and began experimenting with exotic, imported plants from around the world whose proliferation would solidify Santa Barbara's reputation as a garden paradise. These early landowners not only cultivated their land, but began to develop scarce water resources to irrigate their farms and nurseries and sustain their households. In later years, another generation of landowners, the builders of grand estates with their vast, exquisite gardens, would open tunnels, create dams, and build reservoirs to maintain the increasingly lush landscape.

Santa Barbara's attraction to winter visitors from the mid-western and eastern

parts of the United States increased through the years of World War I when European travel was curtailed. Some of those who had fallen in love with the charming town and the verdant hills of Montecito rented large homes or stayed at the Potter or Arlington Hotels, and later bought land for their own home sites. Beginning in the mid-teens and continuing until the Great Depression, these new land owners built magnificent estates in Montecito. They were barons of America's great industries who had already made their fortunes and now wished only to enjoy life and protect their adopted paradise from large commercial and real estate development. Within their own social circle they found talented designers, such as Francis Underhill, Bertram G. Goodhue, and George Washington Smith, who created grand Italian villas, charming Spanish haciendas, and hybrid Mediterranean-inspired architectural masterpieces often surrounded by vast acres of lush and formally designed gardens. The philanthropic-minded owners contributed their business acumen, personal skills, and financial resources to the developing community, and regularly extended their hospitality by opening their magnificent estate parks to the public on certain days.

Santa Barbara's full character was not revealed, however, until the early 'twenties when Spanish Colonial Revival architecture, which had come into vogue in southern California after the 1915 Panama-California Exposition in San Diego, electrified people's sensibilities and charged the architectural atmosphere. With Bertram Goodhue's evocative Spanish Renaissance-style buildings, the exposition helped Californians make a giant leap from the more simplistic Mission Revival style in their quest for a regional identity. In Santa Barbara, influential citizens Bernhard Hoffman and Pearl Chase began a campaign to trans-

form the city into an image of old Spain. They believed that this salute to the region's history not only enhanced the aura of a romantic, mythical past but that the strength and durability of the architecture and its pleasing, timeless design would create a unique identity for the town. Since Santa Barbara had the remains of the Presidio, the mission, the Casa de la Guerra, and a smattering of smaller adobes, the preservationists and developers felt justified in perpetuating this interpretation of the town's past.

Three places were instrumental in the development of the early Santa Barbara style: El Paseo complex, the Lobero Theater, and the Santa Barbara Museum of Natural History.

El Paseo

Developer Bernhard Hoffman, the strongest visionary of Santa Barbara's Spanish recreation, began El Paseo in 1922 as a new town center. His intention was to capture the spirit of an Andalusian village in a new multi-use commercial complex with Santa Barbara's most significant historic adobe residence, the Casa de la Guerra, as its centerpiece. By purchasing the house, transforming it into offices, and incorporating it into the design of the new El Paseo complex of studios, restaurants, offices, and shops, he showed that the city's Hispanic heritage could be expressed in a commercial venture that could be fiscally profitable. Thus, El Paseo became the impetus for Santa Barbara's transformation into a "Spanish" town.

El Paseo, 1922-24
James Osborne Craig, Architect, 1922-23
Mary Craig, Designer, 1922-23, 1928-29
Carleton M. Winslow, Architect, 1922-23, 1928-29

Architect James Osborne Craig's Spanish design is a wonder of narrow passages, heavy wooden balconies, and decorative ironwork. The main entrance, designed as a "street in Spain," links Plaza de la Guerra to El Paseo's large inner courtyard where buildings of varying heights set at different angles create an oasis in the center of the city's busy downtown. At the end of a narrow, covered passageway, a more intimate courtyard opens to the Anacapa Street Arcade. Everywhere, though, hand-wrought iron lanterns, window grilles, and railings complement the pearl white stucco of the recently restored El Paseo.

Lobero Theater

The Lobero Theater is built on the same site in downtown as an earlier adobe structure that was Southern California's first opera house, which was opened in 1873 by Jose Lobero, an Italian immigrant who had moved from San Francisco. In 1922 the adobe was sold, and plans were made to refurbish it, but a structural survey revealed that a new building was in order.

George Washington Smith and his associate, Lutah Maria Riggs, designed the new Lobero Theater under the direction of a committee that included Pearl Chase and Bernhard Hoffman, key promoters of the Spanish Colonial Revival style. The simple, symmetrical design of the tri-level building units are articulated with barrel arches in the entry foyer, gigantic plaster molding, and restrained detailing of the cornices. The breadth of the tile-roofed foyer and adjacent wings diminishes the impact of the larger, taller auditorium and stage house, balancing the composition, while the raised pattern on the stucco adds texture that helps minimize the impact of the large blank walls.

In the classically-inspired interior, huge Ionic columns skirt the edge of the auditorium. Above, an ornate, Moorish-inspired ceiling of stenciled geometric panels crowns the 650-seat hall.

The Lobero opened in August, 1924, to inaugurate the Old Spanish Days celebration and Fiesta. It, El Paseo, the News-Press building, and City Hall stood intact

Lobero Theater, 1924
George Washington Smith, Architect
Lutah Maria Riggs, Architect

Santa Barbara Museum
of Natural History, 1922-23

Floyd E. Brewster, Architect, 1922-23, 1926
Carleton M. Winslow Sr., Architect, 1927-28, 1932-33, 1934
Chester Carjola, Architect 1938, 1953, 1956-57
Carjola and Greer, Architects, 1960
Edwards & Pitman, Architects, 1989, 1995

through the powerful earthquake of 1925. They proved that the Spanish-style construction was structurally sound, and gave impetus to Santa Barbara's continuance of the trend.

Museum of Natural History

The Santa Barbara Museum of Natural History is a cluster of buildings that was begun in 1922 as the Museum of Oology, a memorial to bird egg fancier and collector Rowland Gibson Hazard. The complex rests on the side of a creek in one of the city's most pristine natural settings, Mission Canyon, on lands that had been used by the villagers of the Chumash rancheria of Xana'yan about a mile to the north.

Of residential scale, the initial Spanish Colonial-Revival design by architect Floyd Brewster consisted of a set of small rooms surrounding a central patio.

Although it has grown over the years, the additional buildings have been designed with a sensitivity to the original theme, resulting in a sprawling, yet intimate, complex.

Expansion began in 1927 with five specialty wings designed by Carleton M. Winslow Sr., who had worked with Bertram Goodhue for many years. Then Chester Carjola, and later Carjola and Greer, designed additional buildings in the 1950s and 1960s. John Pitman and his partner Peter Edwards designed the Collections and Research Center in 1989 and the Maximus Gallery in 1995. Although not historical reproductions of the Spanish Colonial style, the newer architecture, with its consistent theme and use of materials, blends well with the older buildings and makes a pleasing transition from the strictly historical to the contemporary.

With the devastating earthquake of 1925, most of the downtown buildings were completely destroyed, and plans for reconstruction in fresh interpretations of historical Spanish style began in earnest. Two thousand building permits were processed by the Architectural Board of Review in nine months.

Santa Barbara County Courthouse

The most spectacular and important project built as a direct result of the earthquake was the new Santa Barbara County Courthouse. William Mooser and Company of San Francisco was chosen to develop its design and manage its construction, and a critical role was played by J. Wilmer Hershey, a Los Angeles architect, who is credited with changing the building from one massive structure to a U shape around a garden.

Santa Barbara County Courthouse, 1929
William Mooser and Company, Architects, 1925-29
J. Wilmer Hershey, Architect, 1925

The courthouse is the glorious centerpiece of the town. The vernacular and Spanish Renaissance architectural elements of this 1929 masterpiece are skillfully blended to subdue its massive scale. Masterfully crafted iron and copper details accent each façade, along with medieval and Renaissance-style ornamentation of carved sandstone and cast-stone embellishments.

The interior suggests a Moorish mosque or palace; it is exotic, and elaborately ornamented to belie its function as a hall of justice. Its most striking feature is the prolific use of decorative glazed tile on the stairs, wainscoting, and floors. Above, highly decorative Mudejar ceilings with Dutch metal gilding and ornately painted borders and wall embellishments complement the colorful tile work. The exquisite law library brilliantly blends decorative elements from Moorish, Gothic, and Italian precedents. And in the mural room, large, theatrical scenes that cover the walls depict Santa Barbara's colorful and sometimes tumultuous past.

The Biltmore Hotel

After the demolition of the Potter Hotel in 1921 and the loss of the Arlington Hotel in the 1925 earthquake, Santa Barbara needed a new, large hotel. The Biltmore opened its doors in December, 1927, and ever since has welcomed visitors from all over the world. Now the Four Seasons Biltmore, it is one of the world's great hotel resorts.

The large complex is separated from the ocean by a rolling, emerald lawn, in a landscape of eucalyptus, oak, and Monterey cypress trees. In these lavishly planted surroundings, the horizontal arrangement of the main building and outlying cottages results in a remarkably pleasant, residential atmosphere that gives the appearance more of a country home than of a large hotel. The architecture incorporates Mediterranean-style design features such as low-pitched roofs topped with heavy, deeply-arched terra cotta tiles, multiple terraces and intimate courtyards, and building surfaces of white stucco that complement the neighboring homes. Reginald D. Johnson's masterful design gave additional, and substantial, credence to the Mediterranean style in Southern California and established the Biltmore, for all time, as a classic. And although successive owners have expanded the hotel, changes have been as inconspicuous as possible, with additions compatible with the original architecture and its exquisite garden setting.

Santa Barbara is unique in the combination of its naturally beautiful setting with its cohesive and dramatic architecture. From the time of the earthquake, the non-urban and historical character of the city, from which its charm and ambiance are derived, has been carefully preserved by city planners, citizen committees, and local ordinances. As a consequence, Santa Barbara has remained relatively small, never outgrowing its topographical constraints. The harbor is picturesque, but is not a great port like Los Angeles or San Francisco, thus limiting shipping and commercial development. The alluvial soil is rich, but since there are not vast amounts of it, a great agricultural industry never developed. The self-interest of new arrivals from the east also helped to maintained the town's small, non-commercial orientation.

But today Santa Barbara is growing again, with an influx of those who are drawn to its special charm. They have added new life to the community, but there has been, unfortunately, a recent shifting from the rural to the more urban. Now, only conscientious planning and committed preservation, of a kind that Santa Barbara has seen throughout its past, will maintain its unique beauty and character.

The Biltmore Hotel, 1927
Reginald D. Johnson, Architect

PART I

Spanish–Mexican Vernacular Adobes

L'Escala Dieu

Casa de la Guerra, 1818–27

Above: Twenty-two-inch-thick, hand-made adobe bricks protected by starchy white stucco allow great depth for window and door openings. Large, hand-made, barrel-vaulted tile roof accurately reproduced from one found in Presidio ruins and a hand-adzed pine window lintel are important parts of this authentic historic reconstruction.

Right: A simple wooden door leads into the mansion's sala or living room. Solid construction protected against the Casa's destruction during the devastating earthquake of 1925.

Opposite: An expansive porch looks out into the Casa's courtyard. Its adobe pillars support a roof of large pine beams, tule reeds tied with raw-hide, and thick terra cotta roof tiles.

Casa de la Guerra, the spreading adobe mansion that faces Plaza de la Guerra, Santa Barbara's civic center, has been at the heart of the town since its earliest days as a Spanish pueblo. Its early California adobe vernacular architecture embodies the romantic and picturesque qualities that were the inspiration for the regional architecture that became famous a hundred years later. The Casa, a state and city historic landmark, has been fully restored by the Santa Barbara Trust for Historic Preservation and is now a multi-faceted starting point for an interpretation of early California life during its Spanish-Mexican period.

The impressive twenty-eight-room mansion was built from 1818 to 1827 as the home of Jose de la Guerra, the fifth comandante of the Royal Presidio and Spanish Santa Barbara's nineteenth century patriarch and most influential citizen. His far-reaching influence in California caused his residence to serve as Santa Barbara's social, economic, and political center for over three decades, hosting the town's important celebrations and civic events and visited by many of the most noted people of the era.

The house remained in the possession of the de la Guerra family until 1922, when preservationists and developers Bernhard and Irene Hoffman incorporated it into El Paseo, the adjacent Spanish-Colonial Revival-style commercial complex that served as the centerpiece for Santa Barbara's architectural transformation into a Spanish town. After subsequent ownerships by various commercial firms, El Paseo and the Casa de la Guerra were gifted to the Santa Barbara Trust for Historic Preservation, which sold the commercial El Paseo and retained the Casa for its complete restoration.

"Casa de la Guerra is America's largest intact adobe residence from the Hispanic period," reports Dr. Jarrell Jackman, Executive Director of the Trust. The scholarly restoration of the Casa is unusual among historic homes in California in that it is thoroughly Spanish. Project Manager Patrick O'Dowd explains, "We have done something unusual in restoring the Casa back to the original Spanish Colonial period rather than the typical 'post-Ramona' period of the late nineteenth century of most of the historic houses in California."

Over a decade, historians including Jackman and O'Dowd completed documentary research while archaeologist Michael Imwalle implemented the physical investigation. Local contractor Ken Ruiz, who is an expert in adobe construction, led reconstruction of the adobe with authentic materials. Materials were worked in the same manner as they were in the early nineteenth century resulting in a strikingly realistic finished product.

Now fully restored, the Casa de la Guerra is open to the public and features a continual program of exhibits on California and Santa Barbara history. In early August, when Santa Barbara celebrates its heritage with the week long Old Spanish Days Fiesta, the spirit and essence of old Santa Barbara are felt the strongest at the Casa. The festivities, food, music, and dance at De la Guerra Plaza, that spill over into the Casa's courtyard, recall similar celebrations of over a hundred and fifty years ago.

The former residence of Don José Antonio Julián de la Guerra y Noriega
Owned by the Santa Barbara Trust for Historic Preservation

The Casa's "bodega," or wine cellar, held large wooden barrels filled with local vintage. Horse-drawn wagons accessed the porch by ramps and unloaded barrels and other heavy storage items directly into the bodega and its adjacent attic. Inside the adobe walls, cool interiors kept the wine at the correct temperature.

Opposite: The living room was at the center of the house. In this main room important guests were received and entertained.

L'Escala Dieu, c. 1940

The rustic adobe hidden deep in the hills above Santa Barbara has been christened L'Escala Dieu (A Resting Place on the Journey to God) by its savior, Serah, a composer and songstress-musician whose busy international schedule makes her life a continual flow between performances in Europe and relaxing at her serene Santa Barbara retreat. The restoration of the adobe, actually an extension of adobe cottages projecting at different angles and levels from a central atrium, has been her focus for the past year. Styled after a Spanish hacienda and built in the late 1940s, the multi-leveled structure exudes a strong vernacular character and appears as if grown organically out of the hillside's own forms of indigenous clay, wood, and stone.

The composition in adobe and wood is much like the music Serah writes, intermingling elements old and new, exotic and familiar, dramatic and mellow. The home's evocative interiors have a decidedly international flavor, with European antiques and textiles, Middle Eastern rugs, and influences from Africa, and resonate a palpable knowledge of the past.

Serah's vision for the restoration has been realized by experts in other fields who work with the same love and appreciation for the house as she has. She found the perfect landscape designer in Gordon Hopkins of the Santa Barbara and Aspen-based Noble Design Studio, who creatively restructured the overgrown grounds and filled the back hillside with a pasture of sweet-smelling lavender, an ode to the French countryside.

L'Escala Dieu, an extension of adobe cottages around a central atrium, has been recently restored to its past glory.

Left: Stairs in the upper garden are flanked by cedar trees and lead to a field of lavender.

Opposite: A view of the atrium surrounded by the adobe structures.

Above: Fine eighteenth-century antiques fill the main gallery, whose walls hold a superb collection of impressionist paintings. Pieces include Persian rugs, a Venetian chandelier made of wood with gesso and water gilt, a rare Louis XV settee, and a Spanish hand-carved mirror over an Italian console. Hiding air conditioning ducts above the bathroom's entry, a hinged bronze grille from Aumont's showroom carries a French renaissance design.

Opposite: A hand-wrought iron balustrade separates the raised open theater-style closet and dressing area from the spacious bathroom below. The bathroom's decor features late eighteenth century Tabriz rugs, rare antique French lace curtains, a reproduction 1920s Italian chandelier, a French provincial mirror over a pedestal sink with a limestone top (once a nineteenth-century kitchen sink in France).

Serah credits contractor Ken Ruiz, a specialist in adobe construction, with the authentic restoration. Ruiz and his crew first spent months scraping old paint off all of the interior wood, restoring its natural finish before masterfully reshaping and restuccoing the interior walls. Under Serah's direction he also crafted new doors from antique imported woods.

Santa Barbara interior designer Héléne Aumont, owner of Europa Design, is the Paris-trained professional who has skillfully imbued each room with the laidback sophistication of the houses of provincial France. Imported and local resources, such as hand-printed fabric from Bartoli Interior Design, were used to shape the feeling of the spaces. When just the right iron or brass detail could not be found, one was specially designed by Aumont.

Her affinity with Serah was immediate, resulting from their mutual familiarity with and love of rural France. Aumont comments, "She is such a good client because she had a real vision for what she wanted and how wonderful the house could be." And Serah, who fell in love with France during her five-year residency there, needed someone who understood the subtle overtones of country French design. Serah says, "I love France. It has heart, and soul, and passion. I think it is the quintessence of the beautiful in life. And I knew that Héléne had that point of reference, too. We had a great partnership. I loved working with her. We shared the same style and taste." The now restored Spanish hacienda seems like a cottage in the South of France. The two forms blend well—their Mediterranean antecedents evidently at home with one another.

The residence of Serah

PART II

The Teens: Italianate and
Classical Designs in Montecito

Piranhurst

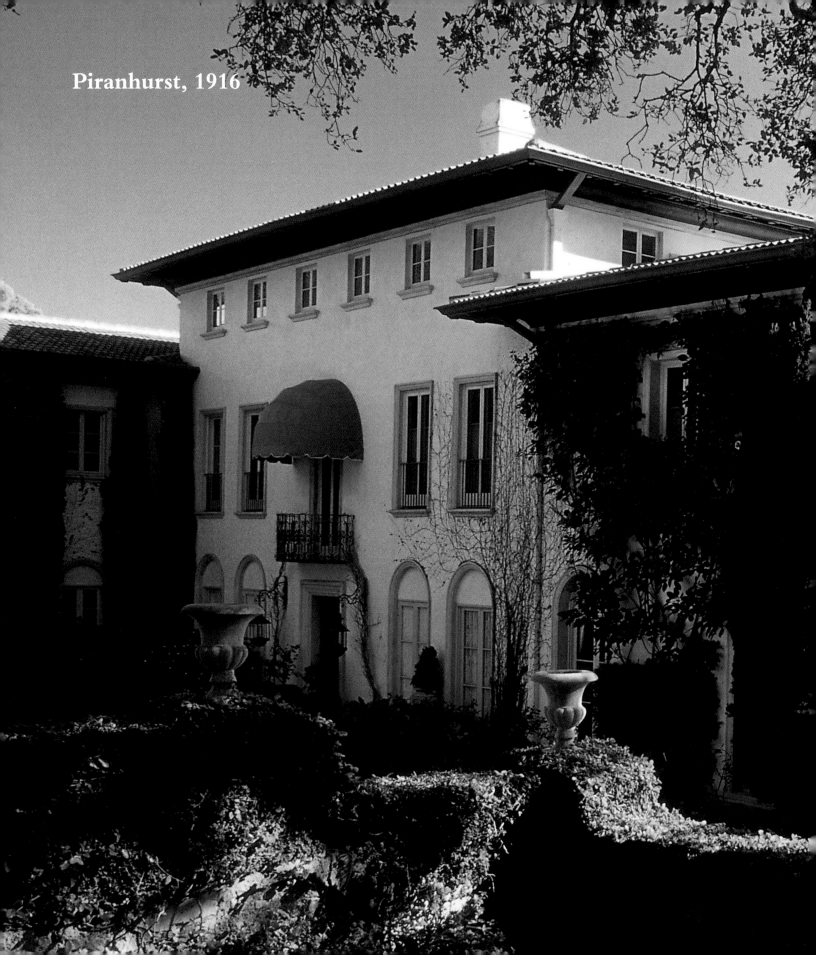

Piranhurst, 1916

The Piranhurst estate, one of the oldest and most exquisite in Montecito, was built during the era when the wealthy constructed houses in the Mediterranean style they had come to appreciate abroad. Most popular were opulent Spanish and Italian designs from climates and landscapes similar to Southern California. Built in the mid-teens as a home for wealthy San Francisco real estate financier Henry Bothin and his new bride Ellen Chabot, Piranhurst is one of the most extraordinary early Italian Renaissance structures in Montecito.

The name Piranhurst (from St. Piran, the fifth-century patron saint of tin miners) was originally given to an earlier house built on this site in 1901 by Daniel Richardson. Although his house was replaced, Richardson created one of the best-planted and most charming landscapes in Montecito. An outdoor "landscape theater," a ubiquitous feature of European Renaissance gardens, was crafted from pruned Italian cypress hedges. It has been continually praised in garden magazines and is still pristinely maintained today.

Bothin purchased the estate in 1910 and thereafter hired New York architect F. Garvin Hudson, who had designed similarly grand estates in Los Angeles, to design an Italian mansion on a knoll with outstanding views of the ocean and countryside. The architectural grandeur of the twenty-room mansion completed in late 1916 resonates in its interior with classical molding details, exotic wood-paneled walls, and imported carved stone mantles.

Piranhurst is seen here from its magnificent gardens, with the Santa Barbara mountains forming a dramatic backdrop.

Opposite: With impressive iron gates at the top of the drive, the classic entry welcomes visitors into a palazzo-style auto court.

Right, top and bottom: Formal European gardens and the California interpretation of English garden elements complement the Italianate architecture. Sturdy live oaks, palms, myrtle, ferns, boxwood hedges and a profusion of wildflowers fill the twenty-five acres surrounding the main house.

Following spread: An unusual oval sunroom opening onto the back terrace and magnificent emerald lawn serves as a receiving and entertainment area.

Top and above: The interior resonates with classical molding, exotic wood paneled walls, and imported, carved stone mantels.

Opposite: In the foyer, a floor of inlaid marble complements the graceful, sweeping staircase. Beyond, the formal dining room is crowned with a sparkling crystal chandelier.

Under Bothin's ownership, the estate expanded to 185 acres. Bothin also later added extravagantly engineered cascading fountains and a cut stone amphitheater in a canyon and a unique teahouse perched on the side of the mountain in back of the house. These exotic features now lay in ruins, their lands long since separated from the main property. Although the estate has been reduced in size, the grandeur remains. The well-manicured lawns and sturdy live oaks, palms, myrtle, ferns, boxwood hedges, and profusion of wildflowers on the twenty-five acres surrounding the main house create the formal European gardens and the California interpretation of garden elements that complement the Italianate architecture.

Today, Piranhurst more than reflects its former glory in the expert hands of its owners, Harold and Annette Simmons, who fell in love with the estate at first sight. "Actually," Annette reminisces, "it had us at the driveway!" The couple put together the interiors starting with a whirlwind tour of the antique shops and grand flea market of Paris. Annette, a talented professional interior designer, continued the search in San Francisco, Los Angeles, and local shops—Summerhill Antiques in Santa Barbara, among her favorites—to complete the lavish decoration. Annette explains, "The integrity of the building and its design had not been disturbed, so there was no significant structural work to be done. I think what we did was to give this lovely house the interior it required and deserved." Annette has transformed the palatial estate into a luxuriously warm home where graciousness fills every room.

F. Garvin Hudson, Architect
The residence of Mr. and Mrs. Harold Simmons

Ca' di Sopra, 1918

The authentic country villa, Ca' di Sopra (House Among the Clouds), was built between 1914 and 1918 for wealthy Chicago industrialist Robert G. McGann, and designed by Guy Lowell, the American master of Italianate architecture. Lowell was trained at Harvard, M.I.T., and the Ecole des Beaux-Arts in Paris, and is best known for his design of the Boston Museum of Fine Arts.

Ca' di Sopra is Lowell's only residential work on the West Coast and was sited in the area he thought most accurately represented the Italian countryside. It is poised beside Cold Springs Creek's canyon and overlooks the estate's terraced gardens, commanding a magnificent view of Montecito and the Pacific coastline. The classical plan of the house is styled after a Pompeiian villa. It focuses on the central atrium, now an open and airy garden space, for which Italian marble was imported for the flooring and carved columns. Views of the exquisite eleven-bedroom Italian country villa were widely published in magazines of the day as well as in Lowell's 1920 volume *More Small Italian Villas and Farmhouses*.

Lowell was also an authority on Italian garden design and collaborated with McGann on landscaping plans for the six-acre estate. Throughout the construction period the architect traveled to Italy to procure authentic architectural details and antique ornamentation for the property's various gardens.

Architectural designer Robert K. Woolf bought the estate in the mid-1990s. He has applied his considerable professional talents, which had transformed Addison Mizner's nearby Casa Bienvenida in the 1980s from a monolithic stone monument of Herculean scale into a dramatically luxuriant palace, to renovate Ca' di Sopra. His design flair complemented by

Opposite: A refurbished steel funicular, installed by its owners during the 1960s, runs to the canyon 300 feet below.

Following spread: Remodeling of the south façade by architectural designer Woolf included a new terrace and symmetrical balustrade staircases leading down to the infinity pool and guest quarters in the lower portion of the villa.

a keen sense of perfectionism was developed over years of working in partnership with his architect father, John O. "Jack" Woolf, in Beverly Hills. He enthusiastically recalls his work in Los Angeles, "We worked with the best of Hollywood—everyone! We did houses for all the big names—Loretta Young, John Wayne, Barbara Stanwick, Judy Garland. It was great fun!"

Woolf has changed the floor plan to include French doors that open the living room to a view of the enchanting infinity pool and vista beyond. He has also added other doorways that create better circulation inside. His redesign of the rather austere south facade with a pair of balustraded stone staircases that lead gracefully from either side of a new terrace patio to the swimming pool below embellishes the area with an appropriate element of classical symmetry. Major relandscaping has renewed the extensive gardens with the formality they had lost under prior ownership. Woolf carefully combined a wide array of California plantings to create a lavish Mediterranean theme that completes the estate. Woolf's Ca' di Sopra continues his exhubertant expression of a timeless and glamorous lifestyle filled with creativity and humanity, and as he says, "It keeps me young!"

Guy Lowell, Architect
The residence of Mr. Robert K. Woolf

Above: Bright, deep colors add life to the formal dining room. Large wall surfaces carry decorative mirrors, prints and plates from Woolf's varied antique collection.

Opposite: In the living room, a Chinese carpet, foo dogs on the mantel, and a twelve-panel coromandel screen add an Asian touch to the large room.

Following spread: The "infinity" pool is surrounded by columns brought from another Montecito estate.

Roman Pavilion (Poolhouse)
of Arcady, 1916

Above: The lower gardens of Arcady estate, surrounding the Roman Pavilion poolhouse and cascading down the lower hillside, became world-renowned during the teens and twenties in garden clubs across America.

Following spread: An addition to one of Montecito's most significant historic estates, Arcady's Roman Pavilion poolhouse epitomized Francis Underhill's sleek, elegant style. Compact in design, it originally housed an indoor heated swimming pool with retractable floor covering and ceiling, changing rooms, and a grand ballroom.

One of the most historically significant of the grand old estates of Montecito, Arcady, was originally built in 1892 by the Richard Radcliffe Whiteheads. The Whiteheads, devotees of John Ruskin, divided their time between their Santa Barbara home and the artists' colony they had created in Woodstock, New York. They named their Montecito estate Arcady and built a serene Tuscan villa in a romantic medieval style to represent the classical ideal of rural peace. Whitehead was one of the earliest farmers to develop Montecito's water sources with the 1,000 foot Whitehead tunnel.

The seventy-acre estate was bought in 1911, and later enlarged to 148 acres, by George Owen Knapp, one of Montecito's philanthropic "hill barons," who set a far-reaching example for gracious living, civic involvement, and generosity to the Santa Barbara community. He expanded the estate as a complex in which to live in a gracious, comfortable manner, where the beauty of the environment influenced a refined lifestyle. Alterations to the villa were made by architect Russell Ray and water works and the extensive cultivation of the grounds commenced.

Fifty acres of world-renowned gardens and woodlands with 397 different species of imported plantings were created by two of the best designers of the era. Near the enlarged villa, the terrace and upper gardens were designed by Carleton M. Winslow. On the lower portion of the property, Francis T. Underhill designed a Roman Pavilion "pool house" and water gardens with a series of pools and stairs cascading down the 1,200 foot hillside past a grotto to the tea house below. Renaissance man Underhill was also a wealthy rancher who had traveled widely abroad and shared a variety of interests, such as polo and yachting, with his cosmopolitan friends in Santa Barbara.

Immensely talented in architectural and landscape design, his work is evident in many estates of the period.

A statement of luxury was preeminent in Underhill's mind as he designed the entertainment and social center below the main house as a Neoclassical pavilion. Its symmetry exudes purity of design and a high note of sophistication. Directly in front of the colonnaded front porch was a large outdoor pool of unusually graceful design. Its outline may still be seen as the border of a garden enclosing a charming reflecting pool. Inside the building, on one side of the entry area, a now-demolished, hot indoor pool had a retractable floor covering it and a retractable ceiling, reportedly the first ever built. The spacious current living room was a luxurious lounge and ballroom. Where a dining room and kitchen now exist, former dressing rooms connected to the entry.

After Mr. Knapp's ownership, the property fell into the hands of owners who modernized it with trends of the period, including the addition of a Mansard roof in the 1960s. The current owner has taken considerable time and care to restore the property to its original classic design. The outcome is splendid and evokes the palatial atmosphere of its glorious past, created by the master of elegance.

Francis T. Underhill, Architectural and Landscape Designer

Top left: In the library, a magnificent wood floor of inlaid exotic woods took artisans almost a year to complete.

Bottom left: The dining room looks out to the pool area.

Opposite: The main entry brings the Neoclassical motif indoors.

PART III

The 1920s: Spanish Colonial Revival and Mediterranean Revival

Miraval

Casa del Herrero, 1922–25

Opposite: Casa del Herero's many Moorish design elements include a series of fountains set on a formal axis and connected by tiled runnels that guide water through the landscape.

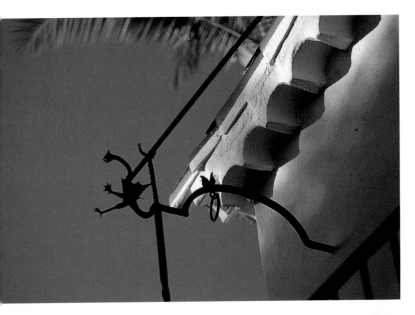

Top: Much of the hand-wrought iron decoration was brought from Spain. When antiques could not be procured, owner Steedman replicated designs and forged them in his studio workshop adjacent to the main house.

Above: An enclosed herb garden outside the kitchen becomes a resting spot with a built-in bench that features colorful nineteenth-century faience tiles.

Casa del Herrero (House of the Blacksmith) is one of the most well-preserved of George Washington Smith's Andalusian architectural masterpieces and has the finest Spanish antique interiors in Santa Barbara. It was designed in the early years of Smith's career and represents a poetic abstraction of the Andalusian farmhouse, a form that he learned in southern Spain and that he continually interpreted during his ten years of architectural practice in Santa Barbara. The Casa is an ideal Spanish Colonial Revival design with a strong Moorish flavor that combines simple and refined lines with an acute attention to detail.

The estate was originally built by George Fox Steedman, a talented amateur designer and avid art and antiques collector who retired in Santa Barbara during the height of the region's fervor for Spanish Colonial Revival architecture. Steedman hired Smith, the leading architect of the Revival style in Santa Barbara and a fellow Harvard man, to help him create a fully landscaped estate in the Spanish-Moorish tradition.

Steedman participated in designing every aspect of the house and gardens, immersing himself with research into Spanish architecture and ornamentation. The Casa's interiors, exteriors, and gardens were filled with pieces from churches, estate houses, and farms in Spain, Italy, and France that were personally chosen or approved by Steedman. Arthur and Mildred (Stapley) Byne, American antiquarians living in Spain, researched and wrote about historic Spanish decorative arts and architecture and acted as purchasing agents for the Steedmans and other wealthy Americans building in the Spanish style, including William Randolph Hearst. They led trips through Andalusian towns that produced the estate's authentic Spanish antiques and

Opposite: The sweeping staircase leads from the dining room to the private living quarters above. A pair of ornately carved antique doors separates the dining room from the entry foyer.

Right: The powder room downstairs is lavishly decorated with colorful, hand-made tiles that the owners had fabricated in Tunisia. Antique hanging oil lanterns have been converted to electric fixtures.

Bottom right: The charming corner fireplace in the master bedroom serves as a focal point, surrounded by Spanish furnishings.

were also instrumental in dealing with the French Tunisian manufacturer of much of the tile prominent throughout the house and grounds. When the Spanish government banned exportation of its national treasures in 1926, the antiques now decorating the Casa had already been shipped to Steedman.

The preeminent landscape architects of Santa Barbara, Lockwood de Forest and Ralph T. Stevens, together with horticulturist Peter Riedel and designer Francis T. Underhill, created a landscape complementary to Smith's structure. During the 1920s, Santa Barbara had an abundance of exceptional residential gardens, but none remains as intact or interprets traditional Spanish-Moorish design as well as that of Casa del Herrero.

The gardens are woven together by water, the essential ingredient of traditional Moorish design, with tiled runnels leading to a series of geometrically-shaped fountains placed at a formal axis to the main house. A variety of garden rooms are created by partitions of sculpted landscaping or contrasting planting materials. In the lower eastern portion, an orchard of orange, lemon, and avocado trees lends a California touch to the lush landscaping, while exotic palms provide a frame for the picturesque view of the nearby foothills.

Through the vision and generosity of the Steedman and Bass families, the Casa is now owned and operated by the Casa del Herrero Foundation and open to the public by appointment.

George Washington Smith, Architect
The former residence of Mr. and Mrs. George Fox Steedman
Currently owned by the Casa del Herrero Foundation

Above: In the living room, architectural treasures of the finest craftsmanship create a rich tapestry of colors and textures woven with iron, wood, stone and tile of traditional Mediterranean design.

Opposite: A later addition to the home, George Steedman's intimate private library is a surprising jewel at the end of a side corridor off the living room. It was designed in Gothic Revival style by architect Lutah Maria Riggs

Miraval, 1919–20

Many of the most significant historic estates in Montecito were built for major contributors to the Santa Barbara community in the first decades of the twentieth century. Miraval (View of the Valley), architect George Washington Smith's fourth Spanish Colonial Revival residential project, is such a place. It was built for John A. Jameson, an attorney who had relocated from Chicago and became instrumental in guiding Montecito's development. Among other achievements, his lobbying efforts for legislation to protect small communities from over-development resulted in the establishment of California's first zoning law, which controlled lot sizes in residential areas. The rural look of Montecito is largely due to his efforts.

Miraval is characterized by Smith's masterful interpretation of the architectural vocabulary of vernacular buildings in Andalusian Spain. His use of authentic materials and command of architectural forms convey a romantic Mediterranean atmosphere. Traditional Spanish design is authenticated by thick stuccoed walls that allow for deep window and door openings, heavy overhangs with carved wooden corbels that throw structured shadows back onto the gleaming wall surfaces, and design elements such as hidden gardens, colonnaded porches, and multi-leveled building units with varying rooflines.

When Jerry and Jacqueline Rubinstein relocated to Santa Barbara, they searched for a well-built family house with both a spacious setting and privacy. Many features of the five-acre Miraval estate appealed to them, but the detail that caught Jacqueline's eye was the small, intimate garden outside the dining room that reminded her of Europe. Often an element in Smith's romantic Hispanic designs, the almost-hidden, enclosed Spanish-Moorish garden with water trickling lazily from a Spanish stone

sculpture embedded in a tiled wall was her vision of relaxation.

The Rubinsteins have altered some of the windows and doors to let in light and enhance vistas and movement. A massive piece of glass in a heavy steel frame is a newly designed front door. The entry hall was opened up and a new multi-purpose room added. Another striking transformation was the replacement of small windows and narrow doors upstairs with multiple sets of French doors. A balustraded terrace on the south facade becomes the perfect place for entertaining with an open-air view.

The grounds of the original estate were laid out by landscape architect Lockwood de Forest. Many of the earlier elements remain, including the estate's stone walls and a section of an historic arbor that once ran for miles along the borders of other estates. The Rubinsteins have added a luxurious reflective swimming pool at the bottom of the lawn near Smith's English cottage-style guest house to serve as the major focal point in the landscape.

Jacqueline has filled the house with an assortment of antiques and new furnishings that create an ambiance that is at once luxurious and homey. Having grown up in Europe and the Far East, she believes, "What makes homes in Europe so great and what people really love, is the mix. The things in the houses are mixed because the families grew up in them and you have a bit of everything. It's not just one thing, which I think is very American, and even more Californian. I like warm, old, new—all at once!"

George Washington Smith, Architect
The residence of Jerry and Jacqueline
Rubinstein

Previous spread: The entry has been lightened with a glass front door in a decorative iron frame. French balloon awnings were later additions. Whimsical tile work around the chimney shows George Washington Smith's penchant for fine detailing.

Opposite: An original George Washington Smith-designed balustrade decorates the light-filled entry. All of the wooden ceilings, doors and windows as well as the terra cotta and brick floors in the home have been fully restored to a natural finish.

Above: The family dining room looks out to a tiled Spanish fountain.

Following spread: Where once an outdoor terrace began, a large room has been added to the south façade. It opens from the main hallway and gives the family a multi-functional space, serving as office, informal living room, and library.

Sotto Il Monte (La Toscana), 1927–28

The formal architecture of the grand villa, La Toscana (The Tuscan), renamed Sotto Il Monte (Under the Mountain), was one of nationally acclaimed Santa Barbara architect George Washington Smith's rare forays into Italian Renaissance design. Smith designed the new residence for Mr. and Mrs. Kirk Johnson based on the inspiration of the seventeenth-century Villa Gamberaia, at Settignano near Florence. Sotto Il Monte's monumentally scaled proportions are reflected in the eight acres of magnificently planned, and now restored, gardens created by Los Angeles landscape architect A. E. Hanson. These exemplary gardens are a California interpretation of formal eighteenth- century Italian garden design popular in the landscaping of the larger, more elaborate Mediterranean estates planned during the decades preceding the Great Depression. These early estates were worlds unto themselves, romantic visions of the far off lands their owners had often visited, and separated from the reality of the large, urban centers from which these wealthy retirees had escaped.

Built with inherited money for an urbane couple in their sixties, this palatial home was designed in a traditional, abbreviated "H" floor plan that provided a large servants wing separated from a formal entertainment wing by a long elegantly articulated entry hall. Open arches of a lengthy loggia with a groin-vaulted ceiling have since been filled in with glass doors to maintain the flood of light required by the interior. A later addition includes a large room that houses an indoor swimming pool built in the villa's style contiguous with rooms on its northern axis.

Sotto Il Monte's front façade is reminiscent of the seventeenth-century Italian Villa Gamberaia, upon whose design the mansion is based.

Top left: Initially exposed, this groin vaulted terrace was later enclosed with steel and glass doors.

Bottom left: The autocourt at the main entry surrounds a large, low fountain.

Opposite: The main house seen from the south lawn where lush foliage surrounds a new swimming pool and poolhouse.

Following spread: A formal garden below the back terrace displays perfectly manicured boxwood parterres, fine European statuary, and a picturesque view of the nearby mountains.

A spacious back patio off the now-enclosed loggia projects a balustraded terrace that overlooks the magnificent formal garden to the east. Manicured boxwood hedge parterres form a pleasing geometric pattern whose axis leads the eye past now gigantic, nineteenth-century plantings of eucalyptus and Monterey cypress toward the mountain-peaked vista beyond. Terminating the south end of the axial hallway, French doors open to a landing that descends to the outdoor swimming pool and pool house, which were later additions to Hanson's original sweeping lawn. To the north of the residence, the green structure of boxwood parterres again organize groups of flowering plants near citrus trees planted in giant Italian terra cotta pots. At the far end, a beautifully carved white stone fountain is the strong focal point for another scenic view of Montecito. Hidden behind tall hedges to the west of the fountain area are garages, gardeners housing, and maintenance facilities necessary for the functioning of this huge estate. To the east of the main garden axis is a substantial pergola where draping vines shade a floor of bricks. Citrus trees, flowering plants, English and Japanese boxwood hedges surround the villa. Monterey cypress and eucalyptus planted fifty years before the formal gardens were conceived, mix with the region's naturally abounding live oaks to create one of Hanson's grandest and America's most notable gardens.

George Washington Smith, Architect

Left: Here, a formally planted rose garden is anchored by an ornate antique stone and iron filigree-work gazebo.

Opposite: The palatial villa's eastern façade is seen from the formal garden shown on previous spread.

Opposite: In the entry corridor, a grand staircase of gravity-defying design curves elegantly upward to the second story family living quarters.

Top right: Carved stone ornamentation and hefty decorative iron lighting designs prove appropriate accents for the voluminous, white-washed interior spaces.

Bottom right: The library is paneled in the typical style of a baronial manor hall, a style George Washington Smith used in many of his houses.

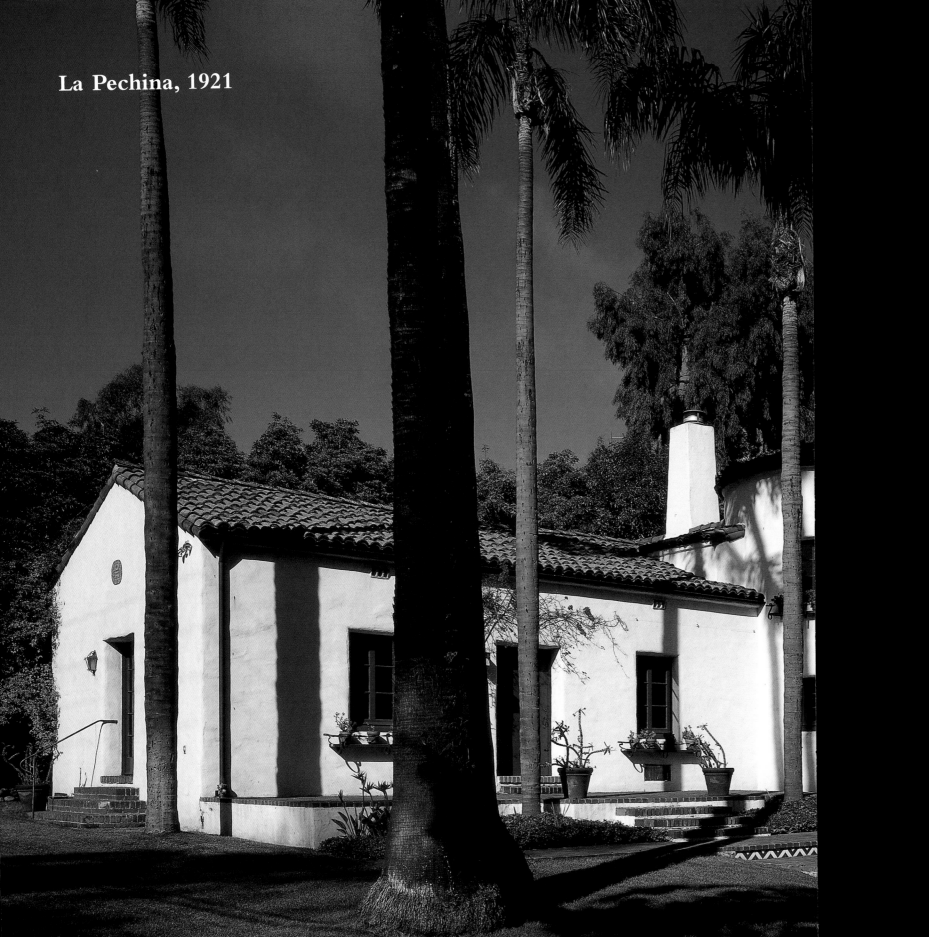

La Pechina, 1921

La Pechina, named after an exquisite Mexican flowering plant, is a George Washington Smith gem built in 1921 for Harry Brainard. The two-story farmhouse with a large one and a half story great room was an outstanding example of a small period home incorporating an open plan with a minimal number of rooms that focused on an indoor-outdoor style of life. Built to meet the needs of a bachelor in the 1920s, the house has since been renovated and reconfigured to meet the needs of its current owners.

George Johnson acquired La Pechina as his residence because it epitomized Santa Barbara and because the Spanish Colonial Revival style lends itself particularly well to a number of styles of interior decor. As Johnson says, "With Spanish you can do anything and it looks good." Johnson's "labor of love" renovation and remodeling took nearly five years. "We redid everything. I mean everything. All that was left was a shell. We even restuccoed," Johnson explains. With meticulous care the original character of La Pechina has been maintained as it has been turned into an intimate showplace.

After discussions with architectural historian David Gebhard, an authority on George Washington Smith, Johnson modified La Pechina with authenticity of the period in mind. A new front wall that provides privacy was added. A gate through this small fortress wall reveals a long tiled bench bisected by a fountain that creates a congenial intermediate space, both whimsical and traditionally Spanish. From here the first breathtaking view of the emerald lawn and the bold architecture of the gleaming white Spanish farmhouse is seen. The house's strongest architectural feature is a rustic medieval tower that evokes a mysterious and romantic past and has been redefined internally as an entry lobby, with a small

Opposite: A colorful tiled fountain and bench create an inviting small entry courtyard and highlight the dramatic color scheme of the house and trim work. The careful detailing of smoothly finished stucco, thick terra cotta roof tile, and an appropriately designed chimney top give La Pechina an unmistakable look of authenticity.

Above: The sculptured quality of craftsman lanterns and cacti plantings lends drama to the rustic entrance of the farmhouse. Architectural elements such as hefty roof over-hangs, thick walls, and deep door and window openings create the trademark shadows of Spanish Colonial Revival design.

fireplace added to the upstairs master bedroom suite, and an unnecessary cistern removed from the roof. The out-of-scale kitchen and dining room areas were enlarged and modified to include details that match the original architecture.

Johnson, who heads an international furniture company, and Dorinne Lee, an interior designer who practices from Los Angeles to Santa Barbara, believe that architecture is an important part of interior design. With Johnson's collections, Lee's expertise, and their belief that good design from different eras can be mixed, La Pechina's interior has become a gallery for museum quality furnishings, including many sought-after decorative pieces from the Craftsman period. The neutral color scheme of natural materials such as stained wood, terra cotta tile, and hand-wrought iron further enhance their blend of old and new furnishings and decorative pieces. Johnson's fine collection of California plein air paintings from the early twentieth century convey what Johnson firmly believes is the reality and essence of California. "If you look at one of these paintings at different times of the day, it reflects what California is all about." The same may be said of La Pechina.

George Washington Smith, Architect
The residence of George Johnson and Dorinne Lee

Right: The great room is now furnished with period and International style pieces that include a sofa by Knoll and black leather chairs by Mies van der Rohe. A Roycroft lamp illuminates an earthy Stickley table and rocker, while beech wood side chairs by Dorinne Lee complement the Eero Saarinen table. A Bertoia sculpture centered on the Gae Aulenti coffee table adds to the scene.

Above: A new built-in cabinet in the passageway between dining room and kitchen displays a colorful assortment of collectible Fiesta ware and Bauer, Catalina, Marblehead, and other Arts and Crafts pottery.

Right: The dining room has been opened, with appropriate period detailing, to provide vistas of the lawn and pool area. Mies van der Rohe chairs surround a contemporary dining room table by Pascal Morgue; a Craftsman-inspired pendant light by Santa Barbara designer Don West hangs above the table.

Lotusland (Cuesta Linda), 1920

The thirty-seven acre horticultural paradise known today as Lotusland began its botanical history as the residence, nursery, and demonstration gardens of R. Kinton Stevens. Known during its ownership before the turn of the century as Tanglewood, the estate was sold in 1913 to George Owen Knapp, owner of the neighboring Arcady. Tanglewood was subsequently sold in 1916 to E. Palmer Gavit, a wealthy New Yorker who had frequently wintered in Santa Barbara. In 1918 Gavit commissioned Los Angeles architect Reginald D. Johnson to design a grand house on the grounds in the Mediterranean style.

The resultant regal 1920 Spanish Colonial Revival residence was set back into the park-size estate, making the eleven-bedroom villa with servants quarters a centerpiece and an anchor for the landscaped grounds. The buildings' proportions and massing are quintessentially Johnson and the ornate Churrigueresque plasterwork applied only on the front door surround, which has since been removed, was typical of his minimal use of embellishment. George Washington Smith later designed the stucco wall surrounding the estate, the swimming pool (now a lotus pond), the exquisite Spanish Colonial Revival-style bathhouse, and the three-bedroom pavilion extension to the main house in the same motif. Its semi-enclosed patio with arches, tile and iron accents, and fountain place it in the heart of Andalusia. When it was finished in 1920, the Gavits named their winter home Cuesta Linda (Beautiful Hill). The unkempt and overgrown gardens were redesigned by Kinton Stevens's son, Ralph, who had grown up on the property and had since become a professional landscape architect, and landscape designer Peter Riedel, who had worked in Santa Barbara with famed Italian horticulturist Dr. Franceschi.

Preceeding spread: Cactus-like euphorbia, clustered and now gigantic, create an eerie and striking image at the house's main entrance. The front façade of the estate's villa is an outstanding example of Johnson's controlled and formal Mediterranean style. With this design, he won one of his many gold medals in domestic architecture.

In 1941 the flamboyant Polish opera singer Madame Ganna Walska, strongly involved in eastern religion, purchased the estate as a retreat center and changed its name to Lotusland, honoring the lotus blossom, a symbol of spiritual renewal. Her acquired wealth through six marriages was invested for over forty years into a passion for gardening, resulting in the restoration and elaborate expansion of the existing gardens. Madame Ganna Walska and her professional mentors, landscape architect Lockwood de Forest and later Ralph Stevens, helped her realize her unique vision for the garden's development with collections of rare and exotic botanical specimens. Strangely wild and tame theme gardens are interwoven among winding brick and gravel footpaths trimmed with lava rock, huge hunks of blue slag glass, and smaller plantings.

The gardens have been considered a phenomenon in Southern California since the Gavit era, and a destination for serious gardening groups. With extraordinary vision, Madame Ganna Walska established and endowed the Lotusland Foundation in 1958 for maintenance of the gardens. They are now open to the public by appointment, and have become her enduring legacy, containing the indelible mark of her dramatic and larger-than-life personality with their grand scale and qualities of exuberance, abundance, and theatrical fantasy.

Above: An intimate outdoor theater based on one at Madame Walska's French chateau grotto was replanted by landscape architect Isabelle Greene and features whimsical eighteenth-century stone grotesques from Madame's French property.

Opposite: The estate's theme gardens constitute exaggerations of the traditional Mediterranean outdoor room. Developed over a forty-year period, strangely wild and tame gardens alike are interwoven among winding brick and gravel footpaths trimmed with lava rock, huge hunks of blue slag glass, or smaller plantings.

Reginald D. Johnson, Architect, 1920:
Main house
George Washington Smith, Architect, 1920s:
Pavilion and courtyard addition to main house, pool, bathhouse, and cottages
The former residence of Madame Ganna Walska
Currently owned by Ganna Walska Lotusland Foundation

Opposite: Three main axes formed of interlocking brick pathways run from the wide back façade through the formal gardens. The terraced garden that leads from the house to the lower open lawn features Moorish tiled fountains, an abundance of citrus trees, and an elegant rose garden.

Top left: Lotusland contains thirty-seven acres of magnificent gardens. Here, one of the entrances is guarded by a newly designed iron gate with a lotus motif.

Bottom left: The Spanish Colonial Revival two-room poolhouse by George Washington Smith overlooks a lotus pond, once the main swimming pool of the estate.

Las Terrasas, 1926

Las Terrasas was the first house built amidst the natural beauty of Santa Barbara's elegant 1920s Hope Ranch development. This 2,000-acre tract was once the site of an extended Chumash village and had always been a favored site for country picnics. Thomas Hope, the Irish sheep rancher for whom the park is named, owned it during the mid-nineteenth century. It later was used as the Country Club of the grand Potter Hotel, providing a club house, polo field, golf course, equestrian trails, and fishing lake for guests.

The business acumen and planning of real estate broker and civic leader Harold S. Chase turned this property into a successful private community. Chase had first choice of sites for his own home and selected acreage upon a knoll to build Las Terrasas. Named for its many terraces on the fifty-acre property, the residence was designed by one of the prominent architects of the day, Reginald D. Johnson, and landscaped by Ralph Stevens, whose designs graced many Montecito estates. Johnson combined and popularized an interpretation of Spanish-Mediterranean design elements with an Anglo-Saxon influence. His refreshingly high standards made him one of the most acclaimed and sought-after practitioners of his era. Las Terrasas was widely publicized as one of the finest of Johnson's projects, winning an architectural award for "best residence of the year" in 1928. As with all of his larger residential projects, its scale and design exude a simple, formal dignity that capture grandness without becoming garish.

Indigenous materials of Spanish and Mexican design fill Las Terrasas. Among these are hand-wrought steel, glazed brick, creamy white stucco, colorful decorative tiles, and thick terra cotta tile that cover the multi-level roofs. Perfect site planning, the expert massing of building units and rooflines, and the harmonious

Right: A tiered stone fountain outside the master bedroom accents the hillside vista beyond.

Bottom right: A stone and wrought-iron wishing well adds whimsy to the pool area of the west grounds.

blending of architectural elements coalesce into a distinguished and recognizable Johnson style.

Both Las Terrasas and his later work of the Biltmore are characterized by long exterior arcades, large windows with full Moorish arches supported by thin steel mullions (Johnson's innovation, which maximized light), charming, small private courtyards surrounded by lush plantings, deep carved-wood balconies, heavy tiled roofs, and creamy undulating wall surfaces with a minimum of ornamentation.

Stephen and Angie Redding chose Las Terrasas as their home because it combined the sophisticated residential style they admired with the amenities of living in Hope Ranch. It is one of the few prominent 1920s homes in Santa Barbara whose original character has been maintained through minimal alterations. Harold Chase even had Johnson enclose the large open loggia in the back so that it could be a more useful space. The Reddings continually utilize this room's airy atmosphere.

The Reddings thoroughly enjoy their historically significant home, and as Angie thoughtfully explains, "We really feel fortunate to live in such a beautiful setting. It's wonderful to be living in a house that has qualities of past eras, some irreplaceable, like the fine craftsmanship in the carved wooden details or a perfect sense of proportion that eludes many modern homes. One of the best things about living here, though, is the sense of serenity, that calm feeling from the past, that's missing in today's fast-paced world."

Reginald D. Johnson, Architect
The residence of Mr. and Mrs. Stephen J. Redding

Above: Hand-carved wooden ceilings in the hall galleria lend authenticity to the Spanish design.

Opposite: The entry hall. Through the large opening, the versatile "in-door/out-door" room, created by Johnson from a former outdoor loggia, retains its original brick floor while French doors placed between the arches enclose the space.

La Cabaña, c. 1880, 1920

Above: In the late 1980s a family wing was projected from the main house that maintained an intimate cottage quality, reflecting the architecture and materials of the original adobe and Goodhue's stone work.

Opposite: The garden boasts a variety of flowering plants, such as iceberg roses, a dwarf Japanese magnolia, silvery succulents, a bougainvillea, a trumpet vine, and cymbidium orchids.

Bertram Grosvenor Goodhue was an eminent American architect whose designs for the 1915 Panama-California Exposition in San Diego ignited California's Spanish Colonial Revival movement. When he was young, Goodhue studied European art voraciously during his six-year apprenticeship with a firm specializing in ecclesiastical architecture. In 1892 he moved and joined a Boston firm later known as Cram, Goodhue, and Ferguson that also specialized in ecclesiastical Gothic design and ornamentation. Having previously traveled in Mexico, his knowledge of Spanish and Mediterranean architecture and Middle Eastern garden tradition was greatly augmented during an extensive international trip in 1902 with his good friend John Waldron Gillespie. Goodhue later designed the 1906 Mediterranean-style El Furiedes estate with its famous Persian gardens for Gillespie in Santa Barbara, and the Goodhues became frequent visitors there and members of its elite social circle. Because of his expertise in Spanish colonial architecture Goodhue was hired to design the Panama-California Exposition.

To establish residency in Santa Barbara after the San Diego exposition, Goodhue purchased fourteen acres of prime Montecito property with intentions to build a grand Mediterranean mansion, but his dream house never materialized. Instead, in 1920 he restored and expanded a nineteenth-century one-room adobe that had been a hay barn for Mexican settlers in Montecito that he called La Cabaña (The Cabin). To make it functional as a second residence he added a second story with a bedroom, bathroom, and an office over the original adobe, as well as a cozy side room with a small corner fireplace, a formal living room up a low flight of stairs from a short hallway off the back of the adobe, a charming cobble-stoned patio, and a

Above: Harris left the stone walls exposed inside; their rough, unfinished quality adds warmth to the spacious new kitchen and dining areas. Old storm drainpipes projecting from the walls were also left untouched.

quaint front porch with shed roof. His construction in adobe blocks with a stuccoed, whitewashed finish and indigenous sandstone maintained the adobe's humble character, with reliance on surface textures rather than any applied ornamentation to convey interest. He maintained this homestead as well as an office and residence in New York until his death in 1924 and is remembered as one of the most gifted architects in America.

Architect Henry Lenny and interior designer Laurie Harris respected the historic intimate cottage qualities and architecture of the original adobe as transformed by Goodhue during their 1988-89 addition of a family wing and kitchen-dining area. They adhered to Goodhue's reliance on the texture of natural materials to set the tone. While Lenny's use of stucco and sandstone visually integrated the design of the new wing with the older structure, Harris's direction for important interior changes also maintained its historic quality. Her splashes of vibrant color are found in a feast of decorative objects and artwork while her earth-toned faux finishes complement the glow of muted natural surfaces. Skylights were deftly added where light was needed most in the large kitchen and dining areas. A dynamic harmony created with the abundance of authentic materials such as stone, brick, stucco, iron, rough-hewn wood, glazed ceramic tiles, and now light, have transformed this historic space into one that is contemporary and exciting.

Original adobe c. 1880
Restoration and additions, Bertram Grosvenor Goodhue, Architect, 1920
Alterations and additions, Henry Lenny, architect; Mahan and Lenny, architects, 1988-89
The former residence of Bertram Grosvenor Goodhue
The current residence of Robert Ornstein and Laurie Harris

La Quinta, 1922

Top: A spacious guesthouse near the main residence, surrounded by luxuriant foliage.

Opposite: Billowy folds of bleached white canvas tenting hint at Moorish exoticism in the entertainment loggia.

Following spread: The estate boasts a three-acre Japanese garden, one of the most exquisite in California.

It has taken a modern artist's sensibilities to reestablish the Mediterranean-style grace of Montecito's La Quinta (the Little Hotel). Diandra de Morrell Douglas, a European-educated film producer, businesswoman, artist, and designer, reoriented the flow of life through her Carleton Monroe Winslow-designed house by an extensive transformation. She restored worn surfaces and tired decorative treatments, expanded the outdoor living spaces, and remodeled the interiors to give the original 1922 home an authentic yet contemporary feeling. Her fine selection of richly upholstered furnishings and her extensive collections of European art and antiques complement the interior's crisp white walls and dark wooden ceilings.

La Quinta was built in 1922 by Carleton M. Winslow Sr., as a residence for Mrs. Robert Y. (Grace P.) Hayne, a San Francisco resident and frequent visitor to Santa Barbara. Winslow was an associate in Bertram G. Goodhue's Boston firm of Cram, Goodhue, and Ferguson, who had moved to California in 1911 to manage the construction of the 1915 Panama-California Exposition in San Diego. He subsequently received many commissions in Southern California, including the eighty-room Bliss mansion, Casa Dorinda, in Montecito. He is known nationally for his Nebraska State Capitol and Los Angeles Public Library buildings. La Quinta is one of this prominent architect's lesser-known treasures.

La Quinta has been changed through the years to reflect the lifestyles of its owners. Parts were first redesigned a few years later after its construction by Edwards and Plunkett, the architectural firm responsible for the downtown Arlington Theatre. The outdoor patio on the ocean-side facade was transformed into a semi-enclosing terrace and a pass-through arch facing the auto court was closed to create a private interior courtyard. Through the years, however, the solid character of the original residence has remained.

Diandra guided the most recent updating of the house and says, "A house should reflect the evolution and growth of the individual or family that calls her 'home.' By this I mean that a home is always a work in progress reflecting an appreciation of beauty and love of its residents. As we grow, our tastes change and become more refined. This should be apparent in one's house. I don't believe that a house is ever 'done'— just as I would hope that its inhabitants are not! I view my life as 'a work in progress' and my home reflects this attitude."

This seven-acre estate is comprised of period Italian gardens begun in 1922 as well as additions made by Diandra, such as the enclosed herb garden, the citrus orchard, and the authentic Japanese garden. Diandra hired the curator of the Japanese gardens at the Huntington Museum, Tom Cox, to help her design the three-acre enclosed Japanese sanctuary. Meandering footpaths and stepping stone bridges, a sixteenth-century baptismal font, a collection of hand-made wooden birdhouses, and koi ponds add charm to the landscape. Lighting and a series of water jets coat the glassy surface of the gracefully designed swimming pools creating a spectacular focal point for one of Montecito's most magnificent views of the ocean and Santa Barbara Channel Islands.

Carleton Monroe Winslow Sr., Architect
Alterations by Edwards and Plunkett,
Architects
The residence of Diandra de Morrell Douglas

Right: In the formal living room seating furniture is covered in silk damask; dark-stained beams add contrast to the massive white walls.

El Descanso, 1922

Cornelius ("C.K.G.") Billings was one of the first community spirited businessmen who gave generously of his time and money to guide and develop Santa Barbara and its public institutions. He derived his tremendous wealth from Union Carbide Co., which he had formed in 1898 with George Owen Knapp. Billings often traveled across the country from New York in a flamboyant style, arriving to spend winters at the Potter Hotel with an entourage of horses, automobiles, and servants in private railroad cars outfitted for a king. In 1917 he bought 104 acres in Montecito to build a residence.

From 1919 the Billingses lived in a Francis T. Underhill-designed Mediterranean "castle" until it was badly damaged in the 1925 earthquake. They then moved into one of the property's guesthouses; the modest proportions and exquisite design suited their needs perfectly. Mrs. Billings preferred the less ostentatious home, and they continued to live there until their deaths in 1937.

Newly-christened El Descanso (The Resting Place), the Billings Guest House was designed with strong medieval overtones in 1922 by Carleton M. Winslow, who was one of the leading architects of ecclesiastical design in the country. The residence, built on an extended linear plan whose central atrium has become an enclosed music room, resembles a complex of church buildings gracing a Mediterranean countryside. Its architecture is embedded with beautiful medieval ecclesiastical elements, chief among them the clerestory stained glass windows of the basilica living room, that define its character and beauty.

After fifty years of alterations in the architecture, the Billings Guest House is again a work of art. Current owners Peter Kavoian and Ray Winn have

Above: The entry foyer and hallway ceilings contain groin vaulting with edges that have hand-painted detailing similar to that found in the churches and chapels of Spain and Mexico.

Opposite: Stained-glass clerestory windows, Gothic style arches for ceiling detailing, and repeated pairs of classical columns add a distinct ecclesiastical flair to the great room.

transformed the baronial interiors to reflect a modern sense of sophistication and luxury befitting the historic architecture and setting. They have also restructured the entire landscaping plan to include more formal gardens near the auto court and less formal planting plans for the pool's entertainment terraces. Architect Henry Lenny, who consulted on the restoration, designed the lower garden with a tiled Moorish fountain to reiterate the exterior's Spanish image. Elsewhere, when the space to install new gardens did not exist, the solution was simple. Kavoian says, "We bought the house next door and incorporated the grounds into our landscaping plan."

Kavoian, an interior designer who understands the history of this significant Santa Barbara house, took cues from Winslow's detailing for the interiors. With a special artistic touch, he designed a mosaic for the entry vestibule floor to pick up traces of light from the antique lanterns nearby. Instead of tile, the pattern that looks like antique stone is actually stenciled with paint. His "wallpaper" in the basilica-like living room is also a trompe l'oeil masterpiece in which an illusion of reflection in delicately repeated images is created by the painstaking process of lightly spraying thinned paint through antique lace. The textured walls have a warmth that is enhanced by the majestic light that flows through the stained-glass clerestory windows rimming their upper edges. The varied palette that Kavoian uses for his brocaded upholstery, sumptuous antique collections, and the ubiquitous extravagant floral arrangements are fittingly regal in an architecture whose ecclesiastical and Gothic references imbue it with an unusual, awe-inspiring charm.

Carleton M. Winslow Sr., Architect
The residence of Peter Kavoian and Ray Winn

Taynayan, 1925

Taynayan is a Mediterranean Revival style residence that really belongs to the exclusive group of grand houses built in Montecito during the 1920s. Los Angeles architect W. Maybury Somervell designed the thirteen-room Spanish Colonial Revival style residence for Louis G. Dreyfus Sr. with privacy and luxury in mind. It is perched beside a canyon to take advantage of the natural beauty of the surrounding vistas, far from the commotion of the city, yet close enough for convenience. Although town neighborhoods have encroached on the site, a thick stucco wall holding massive iron entry gates still provides privacy, and a hand-crafted stone terrace in the back affords magnificent views of former pueblo and mission lands, still beautiful in their wild, uncultivated state.

Dreyfus was born in Paris in 1862 and moved to Santa Barbara in 1886, where he soon became a large landholder. This particular acreage in Mission Canyon afforded him the special opportunity to indulge himself in the history of the Chumash people and his hobby of collecting Chumash artifacts. He named his estate and residence after the village of Xana 'yan (Chumash for rocky place) that previously stood up the canyon from the site. Xana 'yan was recorded in mission records as Janayan, its phonetic spelling in Spanish. The "J" was later mistaken for a "T, " and the word Taynayan evolved.

Somervell's multi-level massing of volumes, at times three stories high, gives the building the appearance of a small fortress. It is planned traditionally around an exterior courtyard, with a central axis entry corridor that unites the first floor entertainment rooms with the service wing. Second story living quarters include a master bedroom that is reached in an unorthodox, but charming manner, from exterior balconies.

Authentic materials, such as stucco, aged wood, iron, and indigenous sandstone and fine decorative detailing with historic Spanish precedence lock the design in the romantic past.

A strikingly beautiful tiled stairway leading up from the entry corridor is the interior's most definitive decorative feature. It is dominated by a series of glazed colored tiles that pictorially depict portions of the text of Don Quixote. Joe Taylor, the president and co-founder of the Tile Heritage Foundation in Healdsburg, CA. agrees with British-based tile historian Chris Blanchett's assessment that, "There is a strong possibility that their maker was Ceramica Santa Ana of Triana, in Seville, an area noted for pottery manufacture. However, there were a number of smaller potteries which emulated the designs of their 'big brother'."

The residence remained in the possession of the Dreyfus family for many years after it was built. Louis G. Dreyfus Jr. retired here in 1954 after a long, distinguished, and far flung career in the foreign diplomatic service. It is he who filled the interior with exotic carved wood detailing and spectacular mother-of-pearl inlaid panels, and designated the formal French receiving room. The current owners, well-traveled, erudite, and also familiar with government service, have restored the internationally flavored elegance of the interior with their spectacular collections of European antiques and art and English family heirlooms. Like many owners of Santa Barbara's unique historic homes, the Smiths endeavor to maintain the integrity and character of the property while enhancing it for contemporary living.

W. Maybury Somervell, Architect
The residence of Robert and Anne Smith

Top: An eighteenth-century marquetry chest adorns a landing in the uniquely tiled main staircase. Hand-painted tiles depicting the text of Don Quixote were imported from Spain.

Above: The mantel fireplace in the living room is original to the house.

Opposite: View from the living room.

Casa Bienvenida, 1928–31

Casa Bienvenida (Welcoming House) was one of the last grand villas completed by Addison Mizner, a bon vivant and nationally renowned architect known for his spectacular residential and commercial designs in Palm Beach, Florida. Practicing there from 1918 through 1928, he developed a luxurious, Mediterranean style that hybridized historically rich elements into a modified Spanish Revival context. The palatial villa on the edge of Santa Barbara, built for his former New York client Alfred Dieterich, appropriated all of these masterful design elements, and in his own words, represents his best work.

During four years of his youth spent in Guatemala, Mizner acquired an appreciation of the Spanish colonial architecture surrounding him and an appetite for all things beautiful. After college studies in Salamanca, Spain, and a three-year architectural apprenticeship in San Francisco, he embarked on further worldwide travels that eventually landed him in New York. During this adventurous time in his life, his insatiable curiosity for the structure and crafting of architecture proved providential for his later career. For thirteen years, his architectural practice catered to New York's high society clientele, but in 1918, Mizner relocated to Palm Beach due to poor health. His Everglades Club, designed in a grand Mediterranean style, was an immediate success that ignited an imaginative spark of exoticism among the resort's wealthy winter visitors. The style proved a perfect match for the climate, landscape, and history of Florida and the commissions poured in. A combination of monolithic scale and evocative elements of Medieval Gothic architecture with adaptations of highly ornate Italian Renaissance and Mediterranean designs characterized Mizner's picturesque architecture. He opened traditional closed floor plans to the many breezes of the semi-tropical climate and added a multitude of windows

Casa Bienvenida was one of architect Addison
Mizner's last works. It is designed in his
trademark Mediterranean style, with loggias
surrounding an opulent patio.

To the rear of Casa Bienvenida, Mizner designed one of his most magnificent Italianate Renaissance gardens.

to capture the sunlight. In the ensuing ten years, he single-handedly changed the character of Palm Beach from a New England-style group of cottages into a unique and majestic Mediterranean-style community.

Mizner lost his fortune in a failed real estate development venture at the beginning of the depression years, and with faltering health, he undertook Casa Bienvenida as one of his last commissions. The house is one of the loveliest grand palatial estates in America, with architecture of the medieval and Mediterranean worlds delineated with force and opulence. Mizner died in 1933 and Dieterich was only able to enjoy the house for a few years until his death in 1935.

The magnificent interiors of Casa Bienvenida, shown here and on the following pages, were created by former owner Robert K. Woolf, who lived in the house for thirteen years from the late-1970s.

In the formal dining room (above) and living room (opposite), the elaborate carved and coffered ceilings are original to the house.

After a succession of owners, the man who brought the estate back to its former glory was architectural designer Robert K. Woolf, who purchased the property in the late 1970s and lived there for thirteen years. He carefully and painstakingly restored the eleven acres of overgrown gardens to the original grandeur of the Mizner landscape plan. Woolf then focused on enlivening and warming up the atmosphere of the voluminous spaces of the house's interior, taking into consideration the interplay of such elements as the pervasive coral stone detailing. "Because the coral stone (cast in Mizner's Florida factory) was such a strong color, we needed to complement it with another strong color, of just the right tone." The foyer ceiling was painted three times until the right depth of blue was reached. The walls of the main public rooms received varying tones of a rich, warm, exotic Venetian red that dramatically enhanced the stone window filigree and trim work. Woolf's eclectic collections of fine artwork and European antiques, reflections of his experiences with the grand homes of England, France, Spain, and Italy, filled the great residence superbly and were the perfect backdrop for a festive household.

In the generous spirit of old Santa Barbara, Woolf regularly hosted Santa Barbara's charities and private social events. He recalls, "That was such a fun period. It wasn't like living in a regular house. It was like living in a palace…Dieterich and Mizner both died within a couple of years after the house was finished. I think they intended that the house be shared and enjoyed, and so this is what I tried to do. What a glorious way to move to Santa Barbara!"

Addison Mizner, Architect
The former residence of Mr. Robert K. Woolf

PART IV

*Contemporary Interpretations
of Mediterranean Styles*

Casa de Los Angelitos

Pompeiian Court, 1999

Michael De Rose is really a painter, but like George Washington Smith in a former era, he keeps getting offers to design architecture that he can't refuse. When De Rose's interest is piqued, it is with a scholar's curiosity that he researches the minutest design details and larger cultural themes of his subject's time period and with an artist's skill that he prepares design drawings and full-scale details at an upright easel. In Pompeiian Court, De Rose's latest masterpiece, his painter's sensitivity and belief that the whole is more than the sum of its parts are evident in his insightful composition of buildings and landscaping of the grounds.

The residence is based on a scheme for an Italian aristocrat's country house. It rests amidst a seven and a half acre agrarian compound on a site formerly occupied by a famous estate (of the same name) that was built in 1917 for Ralph Isham by the Chicago firm of Childs and Smith.

Although De Rose used the same basic floor plan as that of the former house, his interpretation is broader than the original and less confined to a set time. He explains his approach to design as pictorial. "In any artistic expression, what's important is to learn the particular nature of the critical elements, to develop roots in understanding the progression of ideas of a particular culture, and to create a composition that is a set of experiences—items in a context. The task is to shape the set of experiences to create an intangible quality. You reduce the richness of one room to accentuate another. But ultimately it's not the material structure you've created, but the feeling that all of it has together." In the contemporary Pompeiian Court, the flow of the living space from one room to the next has opened up the interior considerably, and De Rose's careful attention to the

Pompeiian Court is a contemporary design by Michael De Rose, based on a scheme for an Italian aristocrat's country house.

Top left: A terrace is off the east side of the dining room, and accessed through its Palladian doorway.

Bottom left: Pompeiian Court was built on a seven and a half acre site once occupied by an earlier estate of the same name.

Opposite: The gardens and small temple off the back terrace.

In the living room, an exposed wood ceiling floats
high above the spacious interior.

details of painted finishes and handcrafted ornamentation has created the feeling of often-illusive authenticity.

The lay of the land guided the placement of the pool and pool house, the formal Italian gardens off the back terrace with a temple structure as a distant focal point, the three-acre vineyard on the southern slope of the property, and the small amphitheater across the creek and winding driveway. A series of five fountains, each of a different style and size, lie along an elongated axis extending from the auto court's center, through the open atrium, to the backyard's outer terrace and formal Italian gardens below. This dramatic feature in unequalled in other Montecito estates.

De Rose says of the two to four year process of building, "It's an adventure because you don't know what the exact ending is going to be. But when you see it after it's done, you know there was a reason to jump off the cliff and that you're going to do it again. Good things can happen."

Michael De Rose, Architectural Designer

Above and opposite: the voluminous bathroom and spacious kitchen follow the precedent of high spaces found throughout the house.

Casa de Los Angelitos, 1990

Above: White muslin shades the relaxation pool, set amidst the gardens that look across the canyon.

Opposite: The sculptured fountain and ring of Santa Barbara sandstone pillars form a dynamic background for seasonal additions, such as the Maypole pictured here.

When Lori Ann David chose Santa Barbara architect Henry Lenny to design and lead her in planning Casa de los Angelitos (House of the Little Angels) in a canyon in the Santa Barbara foothills, she didn't anticipate a trip to Mexico that would significantly influence the year-long planning process. As a result of this trip, the house is filled with references to Mexican colonial architecture that create an unprecedented style and successful modern interpretation of the Hispanic tradition.

Henry Lenny was raised in an eighteenth century Mexican colonial homestead now housing the Folk Art Museum of Tlaquepaque in a suburb of Guadalajara, where he spent a childhood discovering the hidden treasures of Spanish colonial architecture. His designs for modern residential and commercial projects spanning the last twenty-five years exhibit a unique, elegant style, showing his intense love and familiarity with the historical precedents of the many variations of Hispanic architecture. They were greatly admired by David Gebhard, the late architectural historian.

Lenny often takes clients to Mexico to educate them in Hispanic architecture. The expeditions are primarily visual tours rather than buying trips, to experience textures, volumes of space, quality of light, massing of buildings, and the incorporation of architectural details. Lenny explains, "The whole purpose is to gain an understanding of where Hispanic architecture comes from and why." His clients learn first hand about the designs they have fallen in love with from afar. On this particular trip to Mexico, however, a treasure trove of antiques was discovered in an architectural salvage yard outside Dolores Hidalgo. Among them were three pair of worm-eaten wooden doors, from an eighteenth-century hacienda and a church of the same period, that were

later refurbished, set into frames, and now serve as exquisite and unusual exterior doors for Casa de los Angelitos. Lori Ann recalls, " I loved restoring these valuable pieces of art to their former glory. And I love living with these doors. I usually decorate the carved front doors for holidays or try to create a special candlelit entry when I have friends for dinner."

Lori Ann, a dynamic and creative landscape designer, wanted a house that was eclectic in nature and in physical orientation. The various parts of Casa de los Angelitos had to meet a variety of needs, from stables for horses to a yoga studio. She explains, "The house had to be directed to consider the view across the canyon and the gardens and terraces had to take advantage of the sun." This ultimate garden retreat exudes her love for nature in its skillful placement of the relaxation pool, fountains, sculpted lawns, flower and herb gardens, ornamental accessories, and sculpture.

By never settling for a solution at one glance, an unorthodox design was reached that creates a sense of discovery and many delightful elements of surprise. Perhaps this is a result of Lenny's philosophy, which he explains as, "The whole essence of architecture and the responsibility of the architect is to search and find solutions that are strictly befitting to the clients' personalities. As a result, the design is always radically different from one project to the next."

Henry Lenny, Architect
The residence of Lori Ann David

Right: The "hands-on" owner designed the flooring that leads from the dining room into the lower living room; to create the swirl pattern, she inset river pebbles.

Following spread: The traditional Hispanic style guest house/yoga studio is set in the lower gardens amidst colors and textures that form the "sacred space" the owner had intended.

Casa de La Torre, 1991

With its harmonious blending of ornamental and architectural features, Casa de la Torre (House of the Tower) captures the romance and charm inherent in Santa Barbara's older Spanish Colonial Revival architecture. Tom and Nancy Bollay built this quintessential California house in 1991. It is based on the vernacular of Andalusian towns and farmhouses of southern Spain, but incorporates a modern floor plan and design features that update the form and make it perfect for their active, outdoor lifestyles.

As it is such a true rendition of Santa Barbara's unique traditional architecture, Bollay is often asked by prospective clients, "When was this George Washington Smith house built?" To their great surprise (and the amusement of Bollay), they are informed that the house is all new. But while the older houses were often composed of dark, small rooms, this modern residence is filled with light and the formal terraces of the earlier homes have been translated into patios that integrate the landscaped environment into indoor-outdoor living spaces.

Casa de la Torre is a showcase for the architect-owner's skillful interpretation of architectural elements of such 1920s practitioners as George Washington Smith, Reginald D. Johnson, James Craig, Joseph Plunkett, and Wallace Neff. Close study of buildings in downtown Santa Barbara also inspires Bollay. His residence boasts thick plastered walls often punctuated by deep-set windows and doors, an essential part of vernacular Spanish architecture. To maximize light, Bollay also uses large windows patterned after those in El Paseo and the Meridian Studios, where thin steel mullions holding large pieces of glass often form completely fenestrated walls.

Above: The ample window of thin steel mullions, designed to bring light into the north side of the living room, is typical of architect Bollay's work.

Opposite: The entry hall showcases ornamentation that defines Spanish Colonial Revival design: smooth-textured, white-plastered walls; well-crafted hand-wrought ironwork; terra cotta floor tiling; and eye-catching, colorful decorative tiles.

Finely crafted decorative iron details that contribute to the residence's charm are hand-forged, created from patterns carefully researched and reproduced by Bollay. Their design adds another layer of authenticity to the Hispanic design. Colorful glazed tiles, ordered from samples Bollay gathered in Spain, also accent the decor.

A Santa Barbara house's charm and intrigue is often linked to its historical and physical setting. Casa de la Torre is built on a portion of the former Riven Rock estate of Stanley McCormick, son and heir to the fortune of Cyrus McCormick. The grand mansions built here during Montecito's golden era of the first decades of the twentieth century no longer stand, but some of the landscaping remains. Throughout forty years of residency, McCormick continually landscaped the eighty-seven acre estate with the help of a team of gardeners, masons, and engineers. Many of the residential lots created through sub-division enjoy landscape features from that era, including various remnants of its original and massive hydraulic works. A rivulet coursing through the Bollay property is crossed by one of the hand-hewn stone bridges of Riven Rock's pioneering waterworks. Tom's studio is a former gardener's cottage, also of hand-hewn stone, with a charming imprint on its side of the once-attached Victorian glass and iron hothouse. The old stone remnants of the now-gone estate and new design of Casa de la Torre resonate with the history and spirit of Montecito.

Thomas Bollay, Architect
The residence of Mr. and Mrs. Thomas
Bollay

Villa Lucia, 1989

When architect Barry Berkus and the clients who originally built Villa Lucia (House of the Light) traveled to Tuscany to gather design ideas for a new home, they returned with inspiration to build not only a villa, but also a village. A few years after its completion, Jeff and Susan Bridges bought the 8,500 sq. ft. residence and twenty hilltop acres that had been gracefully reshaped by landscape architect Phil Shipley. They have since enjoyed the landscaping of their homestead with its gardens, vineyard, orchards, creek, patios, and swimming pool. The estate is a retreat from the business world of Los Angeles and a private place where the close-knit family enjoys an informal California lifestyle.

Over a thirty-year practice based in Santa Barbara, Barry Berkus has gained international fame for his large-scale, modernist residential and commercial projects across the United States and abroad. In the Bridgeses' home, Berkus's imaginative explorations of the past and modernist sensibilities permeate the design of this villa-village home. Based on the architecture of rural Mediterranean farmhouses and hill towns, this Santa Barbara complex looks as if it belongs in a northern Italian landscape. Some of the authentic architectural elements of villages such as narrow, dark passages and close massing of buildings are picturesque, but proved to be unusable for the residence and needed creative interpretation. To include these elements, but with a twist, Berkus uses height and the flow and orientation of the floor plan along the central axis of the massive, dramatic twenty-foot high great hall to fill the living quarters with light and a sense of airiness. The building units are rotated at forty-five degree angles from the hall's axis so that rooms at once unfold outward toward the grand view and fold inward upon themselves and toward the domestic core. Most of

Previous spread and above: The tower-studio rises above the estate to provide a 360 degree view of the California coastline and Montecito foothills.

Opposite: Earth-colored stucco, weathering under leafy climbing vines, and antique iron lanterns from Italy and Spain give an illusion of age to the villa.

these large, contemporary spaces open to the 270 degree view of the California coastline. This expansiveness juxtaposed with the rustic and antique architectural and ornamental elements of the home create an engaging dialog between the natural beauty of the landscape and the created warmth of the home.

Architect Berkus and master builder Douglas Harris worked carefully to insure that new and old materials were integrated into a cohesive whole. The intentional use of different materials to build the different "historical" segments creates an impression of a rambling family compound or a small village that evolved through the generations. Sandstone quarried on the property conveys an agrarian beginning for the family wing while multiple roof levels and old roof tiles, collected throughout California, reinforce the visual effect of physical evolution. Both structural and decorative beams warm the interior with the fine patina of aged wood. Deep-toned bricks placed in an interlacing pattern on an upper wall or antique decorative tiles set artistically into a corner add additional layers of atmosphere. The ambiance created by myriad historic elements blended into the thoughtful contemporary design give this comfortable family home the imagery and atmosphere for the family's variety of creative pursuits.

Barry Berkus, Architect
The residence of Jeff and Susan Bridges

Above: Informal and rustic Mediterranean landscaping integrates outdoor dining into the oak-laden natural setting surrounding the villa.

Opposite: From the pond-style swimming pool, the home appears as a hilltop Tuscan villa.

Above and opposite: Eighteenth-century French antique floor tiles and cast stone wainscoting and quoining visually tie the main family rooms to the great hall and entry. Antique iron wall sconces and pendant lanterns light the voluminous spaces, adding grace and warmth.

Acknowledgments

I would like to thank James Chen, the talented photographer who poured his heart and soul into this project. He continually went "above and beyond" the outer limits, to capture the spark of magic that each picture holds. His art and perfectionism were inspiring and his professional acumen made working with him a pleasure.

I would especially like to thank David Morton, Senior Editor of Architecture at Rizzoli, for his continual good-heartedness toward me and his positive support of the project. David has been a very important part of my life for the past three years.

James and I would like to thank all of the homeowners who graciously opened their homes and lives to us to make this book possible. We were constantly astounded at the care and creativity these Santa Barbarans showed in their beautiful residences and grounds. We would also like to thank the architects, landscape architects, and interior designers of these properties, as well as the directors, curators, and public relations personnel of the various foundations and public properties that are featured for their invaluable help in research and their commitment of time.

Many thanks also go to the following people who also contributed their knowledge, skills, and support for this project. Their efforts are much appreciated.

Sue Adams, Pearl Chase Society

David Anderson, Co-Executive Director, Santa Barbara Museum of Natural History

Héléne Aumont, Owner; Sarah Stout, Chargée d'affaires, Europa Design

John Barron, Santa Barbara County Courthouse

Douglas R. Bartoli, Interior Design and Environmental Planning

Jon Beeson, Estate Caretaker

Chris Blanchett, Tile Historian and Bookseller (Buckland Books), West Sussex, England

Penny Braniff, Rhonda Harris, Krys Jackson, Hope Ranch Homeowners Association

Kathleen Brewster, M.A., Historian

Deidre Cantrell, Executive Assistant, Ganna Walska Lotusland Foundation

William Capp, Coldwell Banker Premier Properties

John and Gloria Carswell, Northland Development, Seattle

Maria Churchill, Montecito History Committee

Hal Conklin, former Mayor of Santa Barbara

Michael F. Crowe, Architectural Historian, San Francisco

Oswald Da Ros, Stone Mason

Lori Ann David, Landscape Art Design

Mary Louise Days, Architectural Historian

Chris Eberly, U.S. Department of Defense, The Plains, Virginia

Elizabeth Ennis and Merrie Morrison, American Bird Conservancy, The Plains, Virginia

Marcel and Rebecca Fraser, Marcel Fraser Real Estate Broker, Montecito

Ed Galsterer, Marketing Director, Four Seasons Biltmore

Diane Dodson Galt, Executive Director, Casa del Herrero Foundation

Danna Gunther, Research Assistant, Encinitas

Laurie Harris, Interior and Architectural Design

Peggy Hayes, former Docent Council President, Archivist, Santa Barbara County Courthouse

Timothy Hazeltine, Architectural Historian

Kurt G. F. Helfrich, Ph.D., Curator, Architectural Drawing Collection, University

Art Museum, University of California

Maria F. Herold, Montecito History Committee

Geoffrey and June Holroyd, Architects

Gordon Hopkins, Noble Design Studio, Aspen and Santa Barbara

Jarrell C. Jackman, Ph. D., Executive Director, Santa Barbara Trust for Historic Preservation

Michele Jackman, Executive Trainer

John Johnson, Ph. D., Curator of Anthropology, Santa Barbara Museum of Natural History

Kris Kimpel, ASLA, Landscape Architect, Montecito

Jim Knell, General Partner; Vikki Taylor, Property Manager; Karen Twibell, Manager; SIMA Management Corporation

Harry Kolb and Karen Perkins, Sotheby's International Real Estate

Carleen Landes, Executive Assistant, Music Academy of the West

Dorinne Lee, Interior Design, Los Angeles and Santa Barbara

Henry Lenny, Henry Lenny Architects

Anthony Lopez, Renaissance Real Estate

Carter West Lowrie, American Decorative Arts Forum, San Francisco

Nancy Lynn, Executive Director, Lobero Theatre Foundation

Hideko Malis, Owner, Coast Blueprint Company

Marilyn McMahon, Journalist, Santa Barbara News-Press

Shauna Mika, Historian, Los Altos, California

Harriet Miller, Mayor of Santa Barbara

Jennifer Morley, Personal Assistant

Frances and Esme Morris, Delaplane, Virginia

David Myrick, Historian and Author

Bill Newberry, Historic Hand-painted Tiles, Tampa, Florida

Patrick O'Dowd, Chief Curator, Casa de la Guerra, Santa Barbara Trust for Historic Preservation

Katie O'Reilly Rogers, ASLA, Landscape Architect

Virginia Paca, Preservation Architect, South Pasadena

Hugh E. Petersen, La Arcada Investment Corporation

John Pitman, FAIA, Edwards and Pitman Architects

Pamela Post, Ph.D., Architectural Historian

Michael Redmon, Director of Research, Gledhill Library, Santa Barbara Historical Society Museum

Ken Ruiz, Contractor, Santa Barbara Trust for Historic Preservation

Jeffrey Schlossberg, Bulldog Mortgage, Montecito

Kristen Shilo, Assistant Editor

Jennifer Hale Smith, President, Santa Barbara Magazine

Tim Street-Porter, Photographer, Los Angeles

Judith Sutcliffe, Ceramic artist, Iowa

Joe Taylor, President and Co-Founder, Tile Heritage Foundation, Healdsburg, CA

Michael Towbes, Towbes Construction Group

Arthur "Nipper" von Wiesenberger, Style Connoisseur

Daniel Whitcomb, Centerville, Virginia

Resources

Andree, Herb, Young, Noel, and Halloran, Patricia. *Santa Barbara Architecture*. Santa Barbara, California: Capra Press, 1975, 1980, 1995.

Barrucand, Marianne and Bednorz, Achim (Translation by Michael Scuffil). *Moorish Architecture in Andalusia*. Cologne: Taschen, 1992.

Bissell, Ervanna Bowen. *Glimpses of Santa Barbara and Montecito Gardens*. Santa Barbara: The Schauer Printing Studio, Inc., 1926.

Chase, Harold S. *Hope Ranch, A Rambling Record*. Santa Barbara: Pacific Coast Publishing Company, 1963; Mission Creek Studios, 1993.

Conrad, Rebecca and Nelson, Christopher H (Introduction by David Gebhard). *Santa Barbara: A Guide to El Pueblo Viejo*. Santa Barbara: The City of Santa Barbara Under the Auspices of The Landmarks Committee: Capra Press, 1986.

Crawford, Sharon. *Ganna Walska Lotusland: The Garden and its Creators*. Santa Barbara: Companion Press, 1996.

Cullimore, Clarence. *Santa Barbara Adobes*. Santa Barbara: Santa Barbara Book Publishing Company, 1948.

Fink, Augustsa and Elkinton, Amelie. *Adobes in the Sun: Portraits of a Tranquil Era*. San Francisco: Chronicle Books, 1972.

Gardner, Theodore Roosevelt II. *Lotusland: A Photographic Odyssey*. Santa Barbara: Allen A. Knoll, Publishers, 1995.

Garrison, G. Richard and Rustay, George W. *Early Mexican Houses*. Stamford, Connecticut: Architectural Book Publishing Co., 1930, 1990.

Gebhard, David. *George Washington Smith, 1876-1930*. Santa Barbara: University of California, 1964.

Gebhard, Patricia and Kathryn Masson. *The Santa Barbara County Courthuse*. Santa Barbara: Daniel and Daniel Publishers, 2001.

Hannaford, Donald R. and Edwards, Revel. *Spanish Colonial or Adobe Architecture of California 1800-1850*. Stamford, Connecticut: Architectural Book Publishing Co., Inc., 1931, 1990.

Hanson, A.E. *An Arcadian Landscape: The California Gardens of A.E. Hanson 1920-1932*. Edited by David Gebhard and Sheila Lynds. Los Angeles: Hennessey & Ingalls, Inc., 1985.

Hawthorne, Hildegarde. *Romantic Cities of California*. New York and London: D. Appleton-Century Company, 1939.

Lowell, Guy. *Smaller Italian Villas and Farm Houses*. New York: Architectural Book Publishing Company, 1920.

Maddox, Diane (Editor). *Master Builders: A Guide to Famous American Architects*. Washington, D.C.: The Preservation Press, 1985.

McMillan, Elizabeth. *Casa California: Spanish-style Houses from Santa Barbara to San Clemente*. New York: Rizzoli International Publications, Inc., 1996.

Myrick, David F. Montecito and Santa Barbara. *Vol. I: From Farms to Estates. Vol. II: The Days of the Great Estates*. Glendale, California. Trans-Anglo Books, 1988 and 1991.

Newcomb, Rexford. *Spanish-Colonial Architecture in the United States*. New York: J. J. Augustin, 1937; Dover Publications, 1990.

Nichols, Rose Standish. S*panish and Portuguese Gardens*. Boston and New York: Houghton Mifflin Co., 1924.

Oliver, Richard. *Bertram Grosvenor Goodhue*. New York: Architectural History Foundation, 1983.

Padilla, Victoria. *Southern California Gardens: An Illustrated History*. Berkeley and Los Angeles: University of California Press, 1961.

Peixotto, Ernest. *Romantic California*. New York: Charles Scribner's Sons, 1910, 1914, 1927.

Power, Nancy Goslee, with Heeger, Susan. *The Gardens of California: Four Centuries of Design from Mission to Modern*. New York: Clarkson Potter Publishers, 1995.

Singer, Paris and Tarbell, Ida M. *Florida Architecture of Addison Mizner*. New York: William Helburn, Inc., 1928. Reprinted: New York: Dover Publications, Inc., 1992 (Introduction by Donald W. Curl.)

Spaulding, Edward S. (Compiled by). *Adobe Days Along the Channel*; 1957

_____. *A Brief History of Santa Barbara*. Santa Barbara: Pacific Coast Publishing Company, 1964.

Staats, H. Philip (Collected and Edited by). *Californian Architecture in Santa Barbara*. Stamford, Connecticut: Architectural Book Publishing Co., Inc., 1929, 1990.

Starr, Kevin. *Americans and the California Dream, 1850-1915*. New York: Oxford University Press, 1973.

_____. *Inventing the Dream: California Through the Progressive Era*. New York: Oxford University Press, 1985.

_____. *Material Dreams: Southern California Through the 1920s*. New York: Oxford University Press, 1990.

Streatfield, David C. *California Gardens: Creating a New Eden*. New York: Abbeville Press Publishers, 1994.

Thacker, Christopher. *The History of Gardens*. Berkeley and Los Angeles: University of California Press, 1979.

Tompkins, Walker A. *Santa Barbara History Makers*. Edited by Barbara Hathaway Tomkpkins. Santa Barbara: McNally & Loftin, Publishers, 1983.

Vercelloni, Virgilio. *European Gardens: An Historical Atlas*. (Translated from the Italian by Vanessa Vesey.) New York: Rizzoli International Publications, Inc., 1990.

Wharton, Edith. *Italian Villas and Their Gardens*. New York: The Century Co., 1904; New York: Da Capo Press, Inc., 1988.

Wickenhaeuser, Otis. *Captured Dream: A Brief History of The Lobero Theatre*. Santa Barbara: The Lobero Foundation, 1990.

Index